CONTENTS

INTRODUCTION

"It's only by saying "No" that you can concentrate on the things that are really important." – Steve Jobs

Congratulations on purchasing *The Art of Saying No and* thank you for doing so!

How many times have you heard your parents saying "no" to you during your childhood? It has to be plenty of times. You are well aware of the discomfort, rejection, and sadness of experiencing a "no." It is something that you might not want anyone else to experience. That is the reason why saying no might turn out to be scary and difficult. Your ability to say no is linked to your self-esteem. All those people who are well aware of self-love know that in order to be happy, there is no need to please others.

However, there are also instances where not being able to say no might result in outcomes that might not be great for us. Still, most people cannot say "no." We feel that rejecting someone would portray us in bad light or would make the other person feel bad. Also, it is the case that how we treat others is not how they treat us. We end up saying "yes" for a bit of collaboration, affection, acceptance, and consideration. The aim of this book is to make you understand the importance of saying "no" and also how you can do so without any kind of regret in mind.

There are plenty of books on this subject on the market, thanks again for choosing this one! Every effort was made to ensure it is full of as much useful information as possible, please enjoy!

1

SAYING "NO" IS AN ART

Saying "no" is an art that permits us to express our liabilities and freedom to choose and evaluate what we want to do. Keep in mind that saying no is never an expression of a lack of willingness to collaborate. All it helps to describe is that you are determined to stay focused on certain things by determining all that it is better to do or not to do. Do you also find it tough to refuse the request of someone, be it from your friends, family, or colleagues? Do you feel that you might miss something if you end up saying no? In order to say "yes," it is necessary to learn to say "no" at times. It will only hurt you for one time as you cross the boundary of your "yes man." The decision is completely in your hands.

Stay Away From Falling Into the Courtesy Trap

The constant search for acceptance and recognition might stop you from concentrating on all that is necessary or important. There is no doubt that it is positive and is also required sometimes to support each other. You will soon find yourself falling into the courtesy trap. Saying no is rarely linked to any kind of disadvantage. Another prime reason why saying no is so tough for some people is their fear of missing out. You will have to understand that there is nothing wrong with it. There is no need to be everywhere or know everything. It is quite important to realize that you are never responsible for the actions of others and not for what they feel as well.

The Simple Life of a Yes-Man

The life of a yes-man is quite simple. When you try to be a yes-man, you are a selfless and good person. You are famous, stay away from problems, put away your goals and wishes on the side permanently, and rarely taste success as the ultimate result. You tend to live the life of other people. It is never your fault when anything goes wrong. Is this what you truly want? If yes, then you will get stuck in this hamster wheel. In the majority of cases, trying to live the life of a yes-man will work only for some time. Your level of stress will keep increasing with time. Also, there will be an increase in your dissatisfaction and frustration when things turn out to be too much.

The obligations will be out of hand and will ultimately result in unreliability. There will be a risk of you feeling overwhelmed. Your surroundings will get habituated to permanent yes from your side. You will focus on quantity in place of quality. In the end, your dreams, hobbies, and goals will have minimum or zero time. Is this something that you want? As Warren Buffet said, "The difference between successful people and very successful people is that very successful people say no to almost everything."

Learn to Say "No" to Be Productive

When you learn to say "no," you will permit yourself to get involved in projects. It will free you from all those things that might eat up all your time. Being able to understand how to say no is all about blocking unnecessary nuisances so that you can develop a productive space to concentrate on all those things that matter the most. All of us are well aware that we need to say no more often. Why don't we do it? The primary difficulty in saying no results from some sort of societal need. It all stems from the motivation of willing to stay connected to other people. You do not want others to think badly of you. You end up putting a lot of effort into trying to control the impression that you give.

Most people think that they are capable of saying no. However, when the actual time comes, and they get face to face with a person, they end up finding themselves in some kind of embarrassing situation. They just get consumed with lots of guilt. As a result, "yes" is the only answer they can give. You can say that being able to say no tends to imply an emotional dimension. It is the reason why most of us feel the pressure of saying yes to a person when we promise ourselves to say no. The issue is that such a loss of control affects your level of productivity to a great extent.

Saying "No" Is More Like a Choice

There is no doubt that saying no is quite a tough thing to do. It might be complex to say no. However, if you can think about it, it should not be the case at all. All of us have got the right to say no. There is no valid point in forcing ourselves to say yes. In fact, there is no reason for any person to be mad at us for saying no. All of us have got the right to say no, as we have got the right as humans to choose. If you tend to be in a situation where saying no ends up scaring you to some extent, there are two things you need to know.

First, it is a lot more complex in your mind compared to reality. There will be people who will take you in a bad way. There will also be people who will tend to reject you. There will be people who will try their best to make you feel guilty. However, in most cases, if you can say it in the correct way, it will go well. All those who truly care for you will always understand your priorities besides wanting you to be happy.

SECOND, there is no need to worry about what is going on inside people's minds. It is an impossible task to please everyone. If you still try to do so, you are most likely to get lost in the overall process. There will be a person all the time; all set not to be happy with you and criticize you. Do you think it is worth it when you do something you cannot believe in? The way others see you do not matter. Their bad reviews do not matter. You need to live for yourself.

SAYING NO IS INDEED COMPLICATED. However, we all have got a choice. Being able to say no is a choice. An excellent starting point would be to say, "I would rather not..." Try to say this seriously.

2

WHY DO WE STRUGGLE TO SAY "NO?"

"No" – This is one of the smallest words in the English language. Most of us have the belief that it comes with immense power that we are scared of saying it. In all those cases where we successfully manage to say no, we downplay our intentions, offering apologies and excuses to the requestor. Why does this small word tend to have so much gravity? Why are most people so hesitant to say it? The aim of this section is to discuss the common reasons why we face difficulty in saying no to others. You can surely identify a few of them in life for sure. The majority of us were raised in a way that made us believe saying no is egocentric and rude. As a result, we keep saying yes to everyone even when we get frustrated.

We Do Not Want to Offend Others

Most people take offense at things that are not even intended to give offense. One of the primary examples is hearing the word "no" right after they ask for any help. You can surely recall instances when something similar happened to you. Someone asks for your attention, time, or money, and you decline their request in a respectful way. The reaction of the requestor is immediate and something that can be seen openly on their face. A deep frown, a furrowed brow, and tight lips showcase hurt feelings. The person ends up taking offense. In fact, they might say, "That was rude." You will surely feel guilty after this, and that is quite understandable. As you watch him/her walking away from you, the displeasure can be seen in their body language. You cannot help them in any way but get the feeling that you did something wrong.

Let us unpack this scenario in a logical way. It is necessary to understand how this kind of offense comes up to the surface. When an offense is taken in such circumstances, it stems from the insecurities of the requestor. They tend to internalize the "no" from your end in the form of personal rejection. Try to understand that there is nothing to feel guilty about as long as you are being candid and courteous. As long as you can be respectful to the person asking for help, you are not responsible for any offense taken as you say no. Try to do this once, and you can see how liberating this feels.

We Want to Stay Away From Disappointing Others

If you are also like me, you might not like to disappoint others. You hate it when you find out a look of sadness right after your words or actions. Such kind of guilt is unwarranted. You are never responsible for the disappointment of others as you say no. disappointment generally stems from unmet expectations. For instance, you might have visited a café after seeing great reviews only to find out that the food is bad. You are most likely to feel disappointed. When a friend of yours asks for help, for instance, and you are already occupied with your responsibilities, you are most likely to say no. Your friend will get disappointed when they get your refusal. However, is their disappointment your fault? Unless you promise something to someone, you can never be held responsible for their feeling of disappointment. As you successfully acknowledge this fact, you will be able to let go of your fear of disappointing others as you say no. You will get to appreciate that the disappointment is neither your responsibility nor your fault. Such a perspective can provide you the courage to stay away from accommodating all kinds of invitations and requests that come up your way.

We Want to Stay Away From Seeming Selfish

Most of us truly care about the way others perceive us. All of us want to be regarded as caring, good, and helpful individuals. To fulfill this, we end up going out of our way through our actions. For instance, we greet and smile at others, hold the door open for people, and also listen to strange people while waiting at the train station. Whenever someone asks for any help, we say yes instinctively. Doing anything else would seem selfish, isn't it? None of us want others to think of us as selfish. The thought process is quite understandable. However, it is not right. It can easily make you opt for poor decisions regarding how you allocate attention and time among competing demands.

You have got a limited number of hours every day. It indicates that every time you say yes to someone, you are saying no to something or someone else. Every time you say no, you can free yourself to spend your attention and time on some other interest or person. Most of us fail to understand that we neglect taking care of ourselves by constantly taking care of others. You might ignore your family, put your work on the back burner, and so on. Self-care is never a selfish thing to do. In fact, it is one of the most important things to do. The issue here is that you will not have much energy or time to care for yourself when you keep saying yes to others, placing their priorities above yours. There will always be someone who will think of you as being selfish as you say no to them. You can never control that. You are never responsible for them to feel that way. You need to cater to your own needs in the first place.

We Wish to Help Others

Try to think of the last time when you helped someone. You surely felt great. Your advice or actions improved the day of the person. It is indeed a fascinating feeling. It is the reason why we love to help others. Providing help to others might also turn out to be addictive. Some of us search for ways in which we can help others, even when doing so indicates not paying attention to our responsibilities or needs. We turn out to be caregivers searching for people to care for. Whenever someone asks for our help, we say yes. For most people, the desire to help others tends to stem from the inclination to show others that we love them. For instance, you help your friends or family members as doing so is the best way of showing them that they matter to you. For other people, the desire to help might crop up from the impulse of playing the role of a "savior." For instance, we stop to help a stranded driver change their flat tire. There are people who help others as the gratitude they get lets them forget the traits that they do not like about themselves. All such motivations are quite understandable. However, when left unchecked, they can easily make us ignore our priorities and needs. There will be someone all the time who might benefit from your attention. There will be people who will accept your help gladly when you offer it. You will have to remember that you are not responsible for clearing the problems of others. You are only responsible for yourself and all those who depend on you, like your family.

We Want Other People to Like Us

The desire to be liked by others is a universal thing. All of us want others to trust us, get drawn to us, and feel better after they spend some time with us. Such a desire can be said to be hardwired into our psyches. It is the way in which we develop connections with others. We give our best to relate to them and empathize with them. We do things with the only hope of getting accepted by others.

. . .

It is not at all surprising to find out how often we say yes in all those instances when we should say no. It can be regarded as an instinctive response that crops up from our longing for the approval of others. You can say that we try to be "people pleasers." It is one of the most common weaknesses that we all have. There are people who struggle to deal with it even when they do not admit as much. However, it is necessary to understand this kind of yearning for validation as one of the triggers for our habit of saying yes. As you get to be aware of your motivations, you can easily review them and take the necessary steps with which you can realign all your decisions with values. You will need to understand that as you learn to say no with poise and purpose, you will get to improve your overall status in the eyes of your family members, friends, and coworkers. You will be able to gain their respect.

We Deal With Low Self-Esteem

Self-esteem could be a slippery and tricky thing. At times, we get so confident to the point that we feel we can conquer the entire world. Other times, we just feel insecure. You might second guess yourself to the extent that you cannot opt for any action at all. All such feelings can easily affect the way we perceive ourselves. They tend to influence our self-image besides shaping our sense of self-worth. It is necessary to understand this effect as it can discourage us from saying no to others. When you get burdened with a low self-image, you believe mistakenly that your time is not as worthy as the time of others. You assume that your interests and goals are always inferior to the interests and goals of others. With this reasoning, it is no surprise that we get more inclined to place other people ahead of ourselves. Do you know that being able to say no can help in improving your self-esteem? The more you can do it, the more you will be able to understand that your commitments, time, and aspirations are equally important as that of the requestor.

3

IT IS NOT POSSIBLE TO HELP EVERYONE

Turning down an invitation or refusing someone's wish is not that easy all the time. Most of us end up saying yes too quickly, even when we mean no. There are various situations in life that all of us can relate to. For instance, you are chilling on the sofa and having a relaxed time. Your phone rings, and you pick it up without thinking anything. Your friends are on the other end of the phone. They called you to invite you to a barbecue party next weekend. You say, "That is great! I have got nothing planned for next weekend. I would be happy to come." When the actual day comes, your friends ask you to bring your own barbecue set and prepare the same. You didn't expect that. All you wanted was to accept the invitation in a comfortable way. What do you say? "Of course! I will do it."

It is never possible to help everyone in this world. Everything should be in moderation, but helping should always be an exception, isn't it? It is not true, and excessive of it can be bad for you and also the individual you care for. It is now time to understand that helping other people might turn out to be an addiction. It always comes down to the why. Why are you trying to help in the first place? There are wrong reasons and right reasons. You might come up with thousand kinds of reasons to justify it. Do you find it hard to admit all the reasons not to? It indicates that you use up all your energy and see relationships getting affected without being aware of the why. Here are some reasons why you might not be able to help others all the time and be guilt-free.

It Is Necessary to Save Your Strength

Have you ever experienced the feeling of running from one catastrophe to the other? For instance, a few years ago, it seemed like all my friends were experiencing a crisis at the same time. I felt all their pain, and it was an overwhelming feeling. In fact, I broke down for someone I knew barely. What I learned is that it is not possible to be strong always. Is your desire to help others masking some kind of toxic insecurity of being weak? You might struggle to tell others that you could not be there for them as you are unable to do so mentally. It might feel like your inability to deal with stress, and you end up making excuses. This perspective is completely wrong. Most of us lash out at all those we care about as we get exhausted.

We end up resenting all those people we desire to help. It is not healthy in any way, and it is necessary to take back the control as you feel this taking place. They can understand quite well when they care for you too. It can be regarded as a yellow flag when a person keeps pushing you even when you have told them that you need some space. In situations when you feel pressure from various directions, you can try and have a look at the bigger picture. Where to spend your limited amount of energy? You can follow these to manage requests from other people.

- **Important and urgent:** Your friend just lost a loved one and required you at the moment. Such situations should always be placed in the first position.

- **Not urgent but important:** Your close friend is not happy with their job and requires your help to get a new direction. These are the primary instances to explain to a close one that you have a lot at the moment and will be there for them when you get time.
- **Not important but urgent:** A friend of yours wants your advice regarding what they should wear for their date. As you deal with important tasks, you might have to reject all such things so that you can free your mind. The urgency of such not-so-important tasks is powerful enough to suck all your energy.
- **Not important and not urgent:** Your friend calls you to teach them to play a video game. Such tasks are meant to be dropped when you are preoccupied with your own tasks. These tasks can help energize you when you are not busy as there is no pressure.

IT HAS GOT nothing to do with the energy, but it is all about integrity. When helping someone means that you will have to cheat or lie for them, you can easily feel the weight on your chest. Helping other people should be about pushing them higher and not pulling yourself down. It is absolutely okay to move back as a person tries to force you into such situations. You will need to stop supporting a person when you no longer take care of yourself.

When You Are Getting Used

The truth might hurt but not every person out there cares about you. All of us have got a world inside our minds, and we might forget that others do too. For others, you might be nothing more than a minor character who is useful at times. It does not make them bad or evil, as all of us are guilty of this behavior at times. However, when a person does not care for you, then you might need to protect yourself from a one-sided relationship. If you fail to do so, you will give up parts of your life that you could have spent on yourself in a better way or for other people who care for you. A clear sign of you being part of such kind of relationship is when the individual will try to ask you in the first place even before trying to deal with the issue themselves.

YOU SHOULD TRY to help someone when they tell you that they have at least tried to solve the problem first. As you end up helping all those who treat you in this manner, you are most likely to enhance their sense of entitlement. There is no one in this world who can demand your free time other than you. There is no need to be a martyr for people who do not care for you. People who care for you will even talk to you when they do not have any requirements. Such people will treat you as a human being.

Things You Need to Take With You

Not being able to help someone does not indicate you are a bad person. Try to say this aloud, "I cannot fix everything around me."

- **You might be delaying them from getting the help:** Have you got enough skill and time to provide help to someone? If not, it would be better if you could encourage them to look for support at some other place.
- **You require to save your strength:** Have you got the energy to help others? If not, it is absolutely okay to prioritize yourself.
- **When you are being used:** Does the person care for you? If they do not, pay attention to people who do.
- **Listening is enough:** Does the person require your advice? If they only require someone to listen to them, just listen.

4

HOW TO PRIORITIZE YOUR NEEDS?

We all are taught from a young age that being selfless is a great thing. Giving over your needs and wants might turn out to be extreme if you fail to understand its importance. You need to care for yourself and know yourself. If you have the habit of saying yes to everything and everyone while putting aside all your needs, it is a sign that you are not prioritizing your needs. You will have to learn to place yourself in the first place before anyone else.

Why Do You Need to Prioritize Your Needs and Yourself?

Here are some of the reasons why you should prioritize yourself and your needs:

As you feel depleted, you will have nothing to give

When you fill up all your time with responsibilities and keep prioritizing other people's needs above your own, you are most likely to drain yourself of desire and energy. All of us have experienced giving from a feeling of having something to offer – helping a coworker at work, getting our kids ready, doing some favor for a friend, cooking for our partner, and so on. There is a link between all such things and making ourselves do the same activities as we "should." The activities or tasks will be the same. However, there is a shift in our attitude. When you can be kind to yourself and considerate of your needs, you can show up fully to all those to whom you extend yourself.

Doing what you love can recharge you

As you are excited and lit up, you will have more positivity and energy to offer to others present around you. The time an employee uses to rest in place of working all the time or a parent takes off for a date night is not always self-centered. Only because it feels good to you does not indicate it denies other people. By practicing self-care and attending to your needs, you can alter the quality of the way you relate to others. Your friends, family, and colleagues will get to experience you as the fullest and best version of yourself – present and happy.

You fail to practice self-compassion

One of the risks of being lost in all those things that you should do for other people is that you will stop feeling for yourself. It has been found that being kind to yourself while practicing self-compassion can help in the improvement of your well-being. Also, it can benefit people around you. When you stay away from focusing on your needs, practicing self-compassion might turn out to be a hard task. Unless and until you can take care of yourself and your needs, you can never help others.

Your stress can hurt you and the people around you

Your failure to check in with yourself and take out time for all those things that are important to you can increase your levels of stress. Filling up your life with responsibilities can develop a cycle where being stressed might seem like the norm. The society in which we live today, none of us can be apologetic about our levels of stress. In fact, you might make it a habit to wear stress like a badge of honor, proving your value. What most people fail to understand is that stress can take a serious toll on our physical and mental health. Such effects can stop you from enjoying life, not to mention the way it can affect how you relate to other people.

Prioritizing Your Needs

All of us have got our specific set of needs, and all our needs are completely different from each other. Understanding how you can prioritize yourself and your needs tend to go much beyond self-care. You will have to learn to put yourself first and then cater to others by saying "yes." Here are some of the ways in which you can prioritize your needs:

Shifting mindset

You will have to start by shifting your mindset while stopping to think that prioritizing yourself is selfish. It is necessary to help yourself before you can get to help others. As you end up spending all your time with other people, you are most likely to end up feeling stressed and tired. It can make you incapable of focusing and connecting with others. You cannot excel at work, engage with your partner or children, and attain your goals. As you start taking time for yourself, you can feel energized and recharged. You can rediscover all your personal connections. So, simply throw away the idea of saying "yes" all the time and start placing yourself first.

Forgetting expectations

Limiting beliefs are most often developed on the expectations of other people. You feel the pressure to excel in your career, keep the passion alive in your relationship, have the perfect home, and so on. In fact, our parents desire certain things for us. Our partners have their desires and needs. Our friends expect us to be in a certain way and put the group first. In order to prioritize yourself, it is important to keep in mind one thing – the expectations of other people, specifically strangers, do not matter at all. You are required to create your own life blueprint.

Discovering true self

It is one of the easiest things to get caught up in the identities that the world creates for us – parent, boss, son, daughter, partner, etc. As all such roles come to an end – when you retire, when your kids move away – you finally get the time to prioritize yourself. However, you are not even aware of who you really are. The moment you can forget the expectations of other people, you can easily discover your true version. Just stop yourself from thinking about what other people want and question yourself, "What am I most passionate about?" What do you want to do when you get some quiet time for yourself? You will have to recommit to your passions. The moment you start saying yes to everyone and everything, you will get blocked on your journey of self-discovery.

5

HOW TO SAY "NO" WITH GRACE?

Grace and kindness are the perfect ways of saying "no" without being rude. Do you face some hard time saying no? We all know that being able to say no is hard. However, there are ways of saying no without being awkward, feeling guilty, or damaging relationships. Here are some tips that can help you say no with grace.

Switching Out "No" for "Later"

If you are starting out for the first time, there is no need to jump to no straightaway. Saying no is hard. What about saying "later?" It is a lot easier than saying no. Try to make your default response to any kind of request, "Let me get back to you." Let's have a look at some pocket phrases that can be used to extend the "no."

- I will need to ask my partner if we have got anything later.
- Let me have a look at my schedule and get back to you later.
- Great, let me see whether I can pick up my kids earlier from school that day.

- Superb suggestion! Allow me to think about this first, and I will surely let you know about this.

When you are at work, you can ask others to email or text you the requests so that you can get back to them. As you get a follow-up from them, it will get a lot easier for you to send them a nice reply saying that you cannot agree to the request. Make sure that you do not depend on your "later" for your whole life. Also, stay away from lying. As your collection of "later" gets used up, trying to say later again can make you seem to be untrustworthy in the long run.

Rehearsing Saying No

You might not have the convenience of saying no to someone all the time over email or text at your convenience. At times, these requests or invites come up spontaneously and also in person, which demands some answer instantly. In order to prepare for all such situations, it can help you to rehearse your NOs in advance.

- Thanks a lot for inviting me, but I am trying a lot to concentrate on my work these days. So, I will need to say no.
- I am sorry, but I have told myself that I will need to hit the gym tonight. I hope you understand as I want to go to the gym consistently so that I can achieve my New Year's Resolution.
- I have got a lot of things on my plate at this moment. That is the reason why I cannot help you in this instance. I really appreciate that you thought of me for this. Wish you luck in getting the task done.

If you think that you might come off as unnatural or robotic, it can help you if you can rehearse all your lines in front of the mirror.

Not Offering Any Explanation

Presenting some excuse might seem like the best way of declining any request. However, it can easily set you up for awkward situations. Let us have a look at some examples.

- You tell someone that you cannot attend their party as you have no one to care for your kids. They offer you to bring your kids to the party.
- You turn down the invitation of a person to go out for coffee as you have already got some plans for your day. They ask you what day works for you the best.
- You apologize for being unable to help a person with a project as you are dealing with a major deadline. They replied that they would love your help as you get done with the ongoing project.

Despite the excuses that you offer, all those who are determined to make you say yes can come up with various ways of reeling you in. In such instances, you have got three things to do.

- Thank the person for their offer.
- Let them know that you cannot agree.
- Offer no explanation to them.

Realizing You Do Not Owe an Explanation to Anyone

Keep in mind that being blunt with your no does not indicate you are being rude. Even when you do not offer any explanation, it is possible to soften the blow by being appreciative and polite. For instance, in place of saying directly, "No, I cannot do this," you can try to say, "I am really sorry, but I do not have the capacity to take this on at the moment. I truly appreciate that you thought of me. Best of luck with your work."

Offering Alternatives

If the person asking you for something is someone with whom you would like to maintain a positive connection, you can easily reduce the impact of your no by providing some alternative. For instance:

- Your new group of friends asks you out to a bar. Drinking and loud places are not your things. You can ask them if they would like to have coffee or go for some other activity.
- If a person wants to collaborate with you on a task, try introducing them to someone else who might be truly interested.
- A new employee in the office offers to help you with a tricky project. However, you are scared that their involvement might slow down the process. You can ask them if they would like to work with you on some low-pressure project in place of this one.

The primary goal here is to offer a compromise to make sure that the requestor does not take offense to you saying no. Also, it is necessary to ensure that you do not feel guilty for turning down all those requests that might add up unnecessary stress in life.

Using the "No" Body Language

Do you think your body can say no or yes? Based on what you look like, your body can always give out instant answers right before you speak out. It has been found that about 70% to 85% of our communication tends to be nonverbal. So, before you decide to say no with your mouth, you can try to say no with the help of your body.

- Turn away your torso. Try to think of someone you do not like at all who is trying to hug you. You would surely turn away your torso so that you are not required to face them. No matter what you do, utilize your body to signal no.
- Point away your toes. Can you find any pattern? Your feet would tend to point in the direction where you would like to go. So, you can point them away to show that your interest lies somewhere else.
- You can cross your arms. In order to further cut off the communication, close off your chest simply by crossing your arms. It is a defensive and unfriendly posture that you can take to feel guarded.

As you get to signal with your body, the requestor might just get the answer nonverbally. If it is not so, at least your body will make it a lot simpler for you to say no to their requests or invites.

6

TAKE OWNERSHIP OF YOUR DECISIONS

Have you ever felt how simple it is to say "I cannot" when anyone asks for your labor, money, or time? For a percentage of people, the response is more or less automatic. It is like a reflex. There are people who say "I cannot" before they are even able to consider what it actually means.

Not Saying "I Cannot"

In the majority of cases, it is possible for us to help. It is absolutely possible for us to do so. We can give money. We can give our time. We can also offer our labor. However, when it comes to turning down requests, we opt for saying, "I cannot." Such a response permits us to stay away from taking ownership of our decisions. As a result, most of us get into the habit of turning down requests without even trying to express our decisions in the form of a personal choice. It might have some harmful effects in the long term. As you stay away from taking ownership of your decisions to turn down requests, you can never feel empowered with a sense of personal agency. Whenever you say, "I cannot", you keep training your mind to stay away from taking responsibilities. Saying "I cannot" simply implies that you are at the mercy of some sort of external constraint.

WITH TIME, it can give you the false sense that you are not in control. You start having the belief that external factors tend to undermine your authority. You believe that your own decisions are not your own to make. That can be regarded as the complete opposite of being empowering. It is nothing more than being disempowering. You will have to understand that this might have some sort of negative effect on your thoughts and behaviors. There is good news for you. You have got a simple solution to this. When you need to turn down any request or invitation, try expressing your decision in the form of a personal choice. In place of saying "I cannot" to the requestor, tell them "I don't want to."

TRY to provide a reason when you feel that doing so might defuse a combative response. Ensure that the reason is sincere and not any mere excuse. What is more important here is that you own the decision. Trying to respond in this way to all those requests that you cannot accommodate is simply an affirmation of your personal authority and will. You are not putting the blame on any external constraints for the refusal to provide help. You will be making conscious choices regarding the way in which you spend your energy, time, and other resources. Keep in mind that the more you can opt for phrasing that expresses your will, the more confident you can be while turning down requests that tend to conflict with your convictions and needs.

Asking Before Committing

Be it a last-minute meeting with your boss, a drive-by interruption, or an impromptu request, the majority of us try to fit in. We do so by hiding under the layer of being good citizens. We know that the extra commitment has got no place on our overflowing plate. We still end up saying yes in place of no. Try to do this before you succumb to a default yes, start by reframing your way of thinking. Pause a bit before you commit. The main purpose of the pause is to evaluate and understand all that you risk losing. A great way of doing so is by discarding the guesswork and asking for more info.

Being able to ask before you can commit can help you get clear on the sense of urgency that is being put on your plate. A simple query or question to the requestor can help in clarifying the state of urgency. You will be able to take responsibility for what you opt for.

Saying Yes to Yourself

Saying no to tasks, requests, or projects that come at the expense of your priorities are required to be delegated or firmly yet politely declined. There is no doubt that declining is the best option, but it might turn out to be the hardest of all. You will be able to understand that a no to someone is actually a yes to yourself. It is a yes to your priorities and agenda.

7

HOW TO HANDLE TOUGH REQUESTS?

Though there are various kinds of people that you might come across in life, you can always do something to properly handle tough requests. You are bound to get tough requests from people in your life. It can be said that we all experience this. The way you handle it can make all the difference. Here are some of the ways in which you can handle tough situations with ease.

Keeping Communication Professional

When you are interacting with someone from your work or with a client, try to keep your language professional, respectful, and friendly. Your behavior will reflect your business or employer. So, it is a good idea to be mindful of the actions you take. You will need to give your best so that you can repress your impulses to take the behavior of the colleague or client personally. In order to take care of professional communications, maintain an even tone. Also, ensure that you have proper body language. It will let others know that you are open to feedback. For instance, look into their eyes and repeat their name while you respond.

Staying Collected and Calm

Take a deep breath and try to tune into your emotions as you interact with a person who makes tough requests. It would be in your best interest to relax and turn every interaction as smoothly as you can. As you stay calm, you can easily prevent the situation from escalating into harder communication. You can practice mindfulness when you need to deal with tough people on a daily basis. Question yourself, "How are they making me feel at the moment?" You might notice that you are not breathing deeply. Or your heart might be racing. Try to notice the tension that you have in your body and opt for a conscious decision to keep the current situation from stressing out. Keep in mind that your interaction with others will be more likely to be successful when you can recognize and alter your emotions. For instance, when someone gets angry as you turn down their request, maintaining a helpful and serious tone can help.

Giving Them Time to Talk

All of us want to be understood. So, you will need to show the other person that you are listening to them. Try to maintain an open style of body language and nod your head at times. Provide them enough time to express what they want to before you can start responding to them. As you provide them time to express their mind, it can help you understand the situation in a better way. You might feel tempted to speak over them. However, it is always suggested to wait until you can sense a natural lapse in the conversation. If the situation permits, you can let the other person know that you are willing to hear from them. You will need to be silent so that you can absorb everything that is being said.

Practicing Active Listening

Active listening is more like a skill that helps in the improvement of comprehension along with communication in any kind of conversation. It includes concentrating all your intentions on the speaker. You will need to understand what is being said and respond to them in a thoughtful way. The skill of active listening can assist you in understanding the significance of the other individual's words. It will let you do your best to improve the overall situation.

So, you might require active listening when any person requires reassurance that you are paying attention to the conversation. Providing the individual with all your attention will seem respectful. It can help you understand the issue and also how you can cope with it. A great way of practicing active listening is to opt for verbal affirmations that can assure the speaker that you are engaged in the conversation. Here are some examples:

- "Yes, I agree."
- "I can understand your position."
- "I hear you."
- "I am aware of what you mean."
- "It makes sense."

Active listening is something that will need lots of practice to master. It is necessary for daily life as it can help you determine and deal with problems in an effective way.

Speaking Softly

In any situation where the other person raises their voice, it might be the best option to speak even more softly than you normally do. It is better to approach them calmly as you speak slowly. Remember that a calm presence can help keep the situation manageable and under control. Speaking softly is one of the strategies that can be useful to turn down tough requests without seeming arrogant or rough.

Understanding the Point of View of the Other Person

As you manage requests from difficult people, you can take some time to reflect on their points of view. Skills of empathy can always help you understand the intentions or feelings of the other person.

As you practice empathy, it will let you understand the current emotional state of the individual so that you can respond accordingly. It always takes two individuals to make an interaction. In all those instances, when you are dealing with a person placing tough requests, he/she might require expressing their frustration. You would like to hear from them so that you can do something. In order to practice empathy, you can try the following:

- Ask the individual what their ideal solution is
- Nod
- Taking responsibility
- Being respectful

Asking for Support

In certain cases, you might require asking for support from another colleague or a friend. Getting support can help you in various situations to answer questions or to deal with tough requests. Let the person know that you are inviting someone else into the conversation who might help them in a better way or has more authority in accepting their requests. For instance, you can bring your senior into the conversation when a client demands more than you can provide.

8

CONFRONTING FOMO

The Fear of Missing Out or FOMO can motivate you to say yes, even when you lack the energy, time, or money to do so with full confidence. You might cringe at the possibility that you might allow an opportunity to slip away. So, you end up saying yes even when you should have said no. For instance, you accept the invitation to a party only because someone you want to meet is also coming. Or you might accept a huge project at work as doing so might take you closer to your promotion. In reality, the chances that it will do so are quite tiny. However, you end up saying yes as you do not feel like missing out even when there is a small chance. It is said that FOMO is enough to induce anxiety in people. The majority of us tend to struggle with the fear of missing out to some extent. What is more important here is to understand its role in making us say yes without considering if doing so is the right idea. For instance, you might have a chance to manage a big new project at work. You might get inclined to say yes as there is a chance that opting for it might help in advancing your career.

. . .

However, there are hidden costs that come along with managing the project. For instance, saying yes to the project indicates that you will need to say no to other tasks, some of which can provide you with better career development. You will need to consider your availability while paying attention to what you already have on your plate. Do you have the time to take responsibility for another big project? If the answer is no, accepting it might impact your present responsibilities in a negative way.

Slowing Down

Most people tend to move at a faster pace compared to what is beneficial or necessary to their interests. Try to practice and take some time as you drive, eat, talk, or engage in daily tasks. It could help you to place reminders of such an intention in proper places to support yourself. For instance, you can place a sign like "Slow down" in your kitchen. It can work. Taking support of other people, especially with all those you live with, can be helpful.

Going for the Experience, and Not the Symbol

There will always be someone you admire and also envy. It can be regarded as "the grass is greener on the other side" syndrome. Envy might slowly turn into resentment if you fail to determine the opportunities that are available in your own life. Concentrating on the experience that underlines the symbol or object can help you differentiate between what is truly fulfilling from something that will provide you with a temporary feeling. There is no doubt that pleasure is a wonderful feeling. However, it might turn into an obsessive preoccupation that can prevent you from experiencing deeper fulfillment.

Practicing Discernment

It needs to be done in regard to differentiating between what is more important and necessary to what is only desirable. Try to discard some of the things that fail to contribute to enhancing the quality of your life experience. You need to be willing to say "no" to more things. It can provide you with more time that you can dedicate to all those things that are more rewarding. Keep in mind that more is not better all the time. Try to concentrate on all those things that improve your life quality and not the number of experiences.

Being Willing to Not Have It All

Our needs are always limited. Our desires tend to be endless. Accepting the futility of fulfilling all your desires is much wiser compared to indulging in your impulses for gratification. As you prioritize certain activities, it will let you get rid of others. Try to decide your priority list and concentrate on them. Deciding what you want to prioritize will need you to cut off other options.

Savoring the Moment

Try to take more time to linger on all kinds of pleasurable experiences in place of rushing through them to hunt for your next thrill. Savoring the moment will need you to use all your senses for the betterment of your life. Running behind new things all the time will make your life tiresome. Instead of doing so, try to savor what you already have.

Altering Your Focus

Instead of trying to pay attention to what you do not have, try to focus on all that you already have. It is a lot easier said than done. However, it is nothing impossible. Try to add more positive people to your life. Maintain distance from all those who keep bragging or do not support you. The moment you start changing your focus, you can sense a shift in your life. There is no doubt that the shift would be a good one.

Creating the Fun That You Are Missing

Try to spend time every day engaging in all those activities that you think you are missing out in any way. For instance, even when you cannot travel, you can always revisit your old traveling photos to relive that moment. As you take time to take proper care of yourself and address all your requirements, it can help in the reduction of fearful feelings. Try to maintain a proper work-life balance to ensure that you get what you require to decompress. For instance, you could start taking yoga classes if you enjoyed doing yoga on a recent trip.

Doing One Thing at a Time

There are people who are quite proud of being great multi-taskers. The quality of all that you do gets degraded as you do more than one thing at a time. Try to concentrate on one thing at one time and also maintain the same to the best of your ability. It would be helpful if you could make a list of all those things that you require to do. You can also number them based on the order you would like them to finish.

Realizing That You Might Not Actually Be Missing Out

Social media usage has reached new heights in the last few years. However, all we do on social media is always a lot more exaggerated to make our lives seem more fun and better than what they truly are. As you try to think about it closely, social media is nothing more than a reflection of all that we desire to be instead of who we really are. The bigger problem is that when FOMO and social media collide, we might end up comparing ourselves to the exaggerated lives of other people. What most of us fail to understand is that we can never match it as it is not even realistic. Try to stop for some time and realize that the lives you see online do not exist. Can you recall the last time when you went out with your friends, and your best friend frowned in the corner but still posted fun photos on social media? He/she is doing the same thing that you are doing at home at the moment with FOMO for rejecting the invitation to a party. It is always a lot simpler to post the highs and pay no attention to the lows. Always remember this before you allow yourself to get upset.

9

SAYING "NO" IS NOT BAD

You might call yourself a multi-tasker, an over-achiever, or a go-getter. You could be the first one to come forward when there is something that is required to be done. You might handle household duties, coordinate projects, take care of children, and so on. Does this sound familiar? If your answer is "yes," you might be a responsibility junkie. You keep trying to figure out if there is any more time in your day so that you can include another thing, right? Opting for additional duties tends to make you feel powerful, useful, and indispensable. Also, your family might need you, and people always respect you for the kind of dedication you show. That might not be the case all the time or to the extent as you desire.

Not being able to say no or having an addiction to responsibility could turn out to be damaging. In fact, it could mask some deeper issues as well. Getting to find your inner "no" could be empowering. Also, it can make you address all those things that you might have been avoiding.

The Magical Word – NO

Being requested to opt for new things or be in charge of bigger projects might seem like you are being appreciated and recognized for all your abilities. Although that might be the case in certain circumstances, it is also possible that all that is being recognized is the easy "yes" from your side. There is no doubt that people will try to take advantage of all those who are always ready to go the extra mile. As a result, such people get over-utilized. It indicates that in place of getting respect for the dedication you give, you get used to making some other people's lives easier at the expense of your own.

It is true even within your family. Not only that you will be spreading yourself thin within the external duties, but you will also blur the boundaries of responsibilities within your home. The "Of course, I will take care of it" or "I will do it – things would be faster that way" approach will only add more to the plate. In fact, it will fail to teach your family to function as one team.

When you learn to say "no" and reverse the responsibility to all those it actually belongs to, it can help teach them and you. Being able to understand the value of your time is a tough thing to do. Often, the extra project you committed to is an indication that all your other duties will suffer. Your credibility would suffer. You might find yourself cutting down other necessary areas of your life, like your personal life and family, to fit things.

Developing the ability to say "no" to certain things can show others that you have respect for yourself and your commitments. The word "no," instead of being a negative word, can be an empowering and positive one too. As you say no, when it is right to say so, you can show others that you have got boundaries besides having a strong sense of your own value.

NO Might Be Uncomfortable

For most people, saying "yes" when someone asks to do something can feel like the correct thing. When you get asked to do something, it can make you feel that someone finds you worthy. So, whenever you face a situation where you are required to say "no" to someone or something, it feels uncomfortable. You get the feeling that it might make others angry, and you will lose your sense of value. When it comes to your family, saying "yes" might give you the feeling that you are showcasing love. It can make saying "no" seem the exact opposite; something like your family members will think you do not even care.

HOWEVER, it could be the contrary as well. As you successfully deal with the discomfort of making decisions that need you to say "no," you might see that people respect you even more than before. When it is about your family, they might think of you as being more self-sufficient.

How to Do It?

Always remember that determining your inner "no" is all about being able to weigh things carefully. Refusing to do something asked of you blatantly is never a great plan. You can try to consider these before you turn down something or take on it.

- Is it only possible for YOU to do this?
- Is it anything that you are responsible for?
- Is it anything that you would like to do?
- Is there any chance of you sacrificing something – other responsibilities, projects, personal time, etc., to fulfill the request?

- Will accepting this additional duty help you in any way?

Careful evaluation of all your circumstances before you tend to respond is a necessary step. Ensuring when to say yes and when to say no is an act of balance.

Are You Hiding From Something?

There are various reasons that most of us stay away from saying "no" to any sort of additional responsibility. Feeling involved in many things might be tied to your self-esteem. It shows the mentality, "If others need me to do something, it means I am worth something." One more possibility is that immersing yourself in multiple things indicates that you will not need to think of or deal with any other problem in life. In case you find yourself trying to look away from all those things that require your attention using your busyness, all such neglected things will surely find some way to catch you.

No matter what you do to justify your hatred to "no," keep in mind that you might be doing a disservice to others and yourself. Determining the correct balance can be a hard thing. It is more like a work in progress that will take time. When you try to see "no" as a positive thing instead of something negative, you will be able to use it more. You will be able to enjoy all the benefits that it can provide you.

10

WHY YOU NEED TO SAY "NO" MORE OFTEN?

An old neighbor asks for your help to move their furniture, a friend needs help with their new house, and you already have a big project waiting for you at your office that needs to be completed urgently. Even at times when you are filled with work, you might refrain from saying no and opt for doing small favors. After all, you might need to help at one point or the other. We will discuss why this might not be the right way all the time and can damage your overall well-being in this chapter. You will also get to know how to get rid of the yes-man trap.

Yes-Men Live Dangerously

Have you ever focused on so much work from others that you didn't even have the time for what you wanted to do for your own self? If yes, you are welcome to the chronic yes-men club. People who belong to this group or club do not like to disappoint others. Also, they do not want to struggle with the chronic feelings of guilt at times when they fail to help. The main issue here is pretty obvious. When you keep helping others all the time, you will not have the time to take care of yourself. As a result, your health and well-being are left behind. Such a condition will soon result in stress. In the worst case, trying to say yes all the time might also lead to burnout. So, you will have to learn to say no.

Saying no is necessary for your balance and also the balance of other people. It is because this can impact the relationships that you have with others. It is as simple as being necessary for the balance of everyone. It is all about respect. You can assume your position by saying no, and it is always a lot more respectful than saying yes. Try to have the honesty to take some responsibility for all that you think, as it is a matter of respect for yourself and others. Trying to say yes even when you think of saying no is nothing more than a form of flight. Trying to run away or being blind can never solve the issue.

Saying no is also quite important for you to get closer to your goals. Cannot feel convinced? Have a look at your agenda and cross out all those things that fail to appeal to you. You will need to develop the courage to block out anything that cannot give you the excitement you expect or desire. There could be two cases. First, you cross out several things so that you get more time to keep working on your goals. Second, you do not need to cross out anything, and you get to understand that you already have all those activities that can help you progress. It is nothing more than a waste of time when you say yes to stuff that does not tempt you.

NO Gives Value to a YES

Feelings of fear and guilt do not have any reason to even exist. Having the knowledge of how to say no is all about knowing how to maintain your integrity and protect yourself. Having the habit of saying yes all the time can lead to frustration. It often implies an accumulation of remorse or regrets, none of which is great for your self-esteem.

. . .

Accepting requests from others will surely please them. You will be regarded as non-confrontational and pleasant. However, it will slowly result in annoyance because of a lack of assertiveness. You might end up losing your credibility quite quickly besides gaining a bad reputation among others. It can lead to stress that will ultimately affect your health condition. You will have to understand that a genuine no will give more value to the yes.

Questions to Ask

You will need to start by establishing your goals and limits. What are you prepared to do for other people? What are the requests that you can always accept? You will have to make sure that the response is coherent with the professional objectives. Is it good for your career? Will you get penalized if you say no? Do you have the time to provide help to others despite your workload? The answers, negative or positive, will turn out to be evident as the reflection gets completed. A reflection on the professional and personal plan permits reaching a response that is better adapted to the needs and desires and much less to that of other people.

Reasons to Say NO More Often

Here are some of the reasons that can help you say "no" more often:

Saying No won't make you selfish

There are people who are unable to say no as they think it is more like being selfish to take time for themselves. However, you will need to understand that a true selfish individual will never feel any guilt while saying no.

. . .

It is not possible to please everyone

It is completely okay to please all those who are close to you or your love once in a while. However, it is more like an impossible task to keep everyone happy all the time. You might have the idea that you cannot disappoint anyone. Soon you will not even have the choice to disappoint when you want to be respected and to prevent other people from abusing your kindness. When anyone gets the idea that you say yes to everything, they are most likely to make it a habit to take advantage of you.

Saying No is not going to hurt your connections

You might have the fear that when you say no to someone, they will not talk to you any longer. If you cannot say no as you are scared that the other individual will leave you or judge you, there is no doubt that the relationship is toxic and imbalanced. It will be better for you if you can get rid of it as soon as possible.

You will need to understand that moving away from a person is a lot better than being in an unhealthy situation, regardless of what the other person tries to tell you. Anyone who genuinely loves you and cares for you will always try to respect your limits. They can understand the reasons behind your refusal.

Saying No is about giving more time to yourself to enjoy life more

As you say no to all those things that take away a great deal of your responsibility and time, you will be saying yes to various things that can enrich your life. You will say yes to good times with family, friends, or your partner. You will be saying yes to having more time for yourself, your hobbies, and maintaining your sanity.

SAYING No can protect you from manipulators

PEOPLE WHO ARE experts in manipulation opt for various tactics that can make you say yes. There are manipulators who opt for bullying and insist you do something that you do not want to do with an aggressive or mean attitude. Some might take up the victim role and keep complaining until you decide to give in. Some people might try to make you feel guilty.

ALSO, there are people who might compliment you and then ask for what they need. Try not to give in to such manipulative techniques. Never agree to do anything only because you are getting pressured to do so. At times, they could be your loved ones, and they will accept your refusal. In other instances, it will take you away from all those people who keep trying to take advantage of you.

11

BOUNDARIES AND SELF-ESTEEM

Your work desk is full of papers, and your everyday to-do list has a lot more than what you can manage. Your boss calls you and asks you to get done with an urgent task. You might like to say no in such situations; however, you find it difficult. Most people cannot understand that a no can also offer lots of advantages. It is all about your self-esteem, boundaries, and how you respect them.

Saying "No" All the Time Comes With Risks

Saying no when required is important as when you keep loading yourself up with more tasks, you will run the risk of overloading yourself. It can easily hamper the quality of how you work, along with your mental and physical state. It has been found that most people tend to work even worse when they function under excessive pressure.

Your colleagues, seniors, friends, or even family members might get the impression that you are available all the time. So, they might try to offload all kinds of unpleasant tasks for you. In fact, they might not accept when you try to say no to their request later. It can very easily affect your self-confidence. All those who try to sacrifice themselves for other people end up forgetting their own needs. What you need to do is set your limits or boundaries.

Why Is It Tough to Set Limits?

If you are unable to say no, the chances are high that you are scared of other people taking it negatively. You might fear that you will be perceived as inflexible, unfriendly, selfish, lazy, or overwhelmed. However, a bit of change in perspective can help a lot here. How do you feel when a colleague cannot support you? Do you have negative feelings towards them? Probably not, and it is also true that your colleague will also not do that either. Another common reason is increased perfectionism or an unhealthy self-perception. It might be the case that you have high demands on your own performance. You desire to do everything and end up overwhelming yourself.

YOUR SELF-WORTH SHOULD NEVER BE dependent on your performance alone. On the contrary, you are responsible for the management of your resources and communicating when you are not able to do something more. It can prevent overload or possible burnout.

What Do Limits Mean in Relation to Self-Esteem?

Setting, perceiving, and respecting boundaries are necessary skills in developing and regulating healthy self-esteem. There will always be conflicts, failures, problems, or crises in life that will affect you and challenge you. Emotional injuries, disappointments, and losses can very easily affect your self-esteem. A healthy internal boundary can help strengthen your autonomy. Every kind of independence can boost your self-worth. A clear yes and clear no can show both the inward and outward boundaries.

. . .

All of us require our own space. It includes all that we are with our values, needs, and abilities. We are not that well connected with our parts most of the time. For instance, most of us are busy fulfilling other people's expectations in place of paying attention to our requirements. In fact, our inner critic might come up and make us doubt ourselves.

However, having healthy boundaries can make things clear about who you are and who you are not. You can always set yourself apart without feeling guilty and going your own way. The more harmoniously you can live, the higher your self-worth will be. There will be no need to compare yourself anymore as you will get to live for yourself and also be satisfied with the same.

Tips to Set Your Limits

It is always a positive thing when you can identify yourself with your work while being passionate about it. However, you will need to place your needs above that of others. Here are some tips that can help you set your limits with ease.

Offering alternatives

You might find it a lot easier to say no when you suggest an alternative option or solution simultaneously. For instance, you can say, "Unfortunately, I won't be able to help you with your shifting, but I can ask a friend of mine to help you." Or you can say, "I will need to do a lot of hard work for this project. I will surely think about it whether I can be a part of it."

. . .

Clear communication

There are people who tend to feel guilty for saying no. At times, you might end up apologizing, and that too, in an awkward way, when you reject someone's request. You should not do this as it will put you up in a defensive position. In place of doing so, try to communicate the 'no' from your side in a firm and friendly way. It will never offend the other person. Also, when you set your limits and be aware of the same, others will respect them too.

The magical Cs

If you fail to say no, there are people who might tend to take advantage of you. You can get great protection against this with the help of proper communication and also by using the three Cs.

- Communicate what you feel – unfair treatment, stressed, etc.
- Communicate all that you desire for the future – "Let us get in touch earlier the next time and distribute the work in a better way."
- Communicate the effect – "I am overloaded, and I am unable to deal with my core business."

Separating **free time and work**

Your constant availability can never make it easier for you to say no. You might tend to reply to your work emails even when you are not working or at times when you are with your family. Most people fail to understand the danger that is lurking here. When you cannot differentiate between leisure and work, you might not be able to do both. In place of doing so, you can inform others, like your colleagues, when you can be reached. Try to stick to this as much as you can and maintain your limits.

Making them set priorities

When you find it hard to say no to someone, like your boss, you can opt for a little trick here. You can say, "I will be glad to take up this project. However, I also have got the following things to do. Which task do you think is more important here? I will work according to that only." Now, the ball is in their area, and they are the ones who will need to make a decision. Try to make it transparent which duties or tasks you have waiting for you ahead.

Keep practicing

As with every other thing in life, setting your limits can get easier with some practice from your side. When you start, you might experience palpitations or clammy hands as you refuse someone's request. Trust me, it will get easier with time. Saying no will not hurt anyone when it is for your good. You will get to earn more respect from others instead of simply accepting everything that comes up your way.

12

THE BENEFITS OF SAYING "NO"

Do you belong to the group of "yes" sayers? You nod to every request of your boss, family, friends, or colleagues. Saying no might not be that easy all the time, specifically with those you love or care for. There are certain benefits of saying no that can make it easier for you to say so. Most people are influenced to think that saying yes is the right thing; however, that is not the case. All of us are programmed to think of saying no as a negative thing and saying yes as a positive one. Let's have a look at some of the benefits of saying no.

Permits You to Be Honest

Saying no will let you be honest about all that you feel. If you really do not want to be a part of the project or do not want to go to the party, you will have to speak up. Try to tell no to others as you have other commitments. Never feel guilty about saying no or have the notion that you owe a brief explanation to the other person. Offering a simple thank you for the invite followed by declining the same as you have to deal with other commitments can do the trick.

Empowers You

There are people who are forced to participate in projects or events as they cannot say no to the requestor. All of us want to please others. However, courtesy can get you only so far before you resent yourself and the other person for making you do all those things that you do not want to. As you say no, it is about giving importance to your needs and feelings. It can be quite empowering. Being able to say no can support you in developing your confidence in the long term. It can empower you to take control of time and, in the end, the course of life.

Leaves Space to Concentrate on Priorities

When you build the habit of saying yes to helping out or doing side projects, you will be missing out on your priorities. Being able to say no will free up time that will let you concentrate on your priority list. Excessive interruptions at work can easily hamper your task flow, and it will take you time to get back to your initial spot.

If you want to make a proper impact at home and work, you will have to start by concentrating on all your priorities right before you can say yes to other people. It might indicate saying no to providing help to a colleague again who keeps starting their projects at the last minute and saying yes to the hiking plan that you have already planned the last month.

Means Yes to Other Things

There are people who are quite afraid of saying no as they feel scared of missing out on things. It is an incorrect perception. Being able to say no to all those things you are not passionate about means leaving space to say yes to all those things you want or like to participate in. So, the next time when you find yourself willing to say yes as you do not want to miss out, try to remind yourself that saying no is about saying yes to other things in the future.

Provides a Chance to Others to Say Yes

As you say no, it will permit others to step up and opt for a new challenge. In this way, you will provide an opportunity for others to grow as you concentrate on your priorities. It can be said that it will be a win-win situation for all.

13

PAY RESPECT TO YOUR TIME

Do you feel that you never get enough time for yourself? It could be the case when you keep saying yes to everyone and everything. Time is precious. You can never get back the time that is already spent. You will need to respect your time to respect yourself. Thinking about how you can take charge of your schedule and time? Here are some of the ways in which you can do so.

Evaluating Your Schedule Honestly

Try to take a hard look at your schedule for the next few days. What can you see? How is your schedule set up as a whole? Is your schedule in line with your interests and goals? Do you think you have more items on the schedule that are meant for others rather than your well-being and interests? In case it is so, you will need to change your schedule. Make sure the schedule you follow is in line with you in the first place, and then come to other people.

Putting Yourself First

As you put yourself first in your schedule, it will show that you dedicate time for your own self. Life is too short to waste any time. Try to act accordingly and make sure to schedule as much time as you can for yourself. Use your "me" time for meditation, relaxation, exercise, watching your favorite show, playing with your pet dog, reading books, or anything that you want to do with your time.

Streamlining Time Spent With Other People

Do you need to meet someone in person, or is it possible to solve the problem in a time-efficient manner, like through an email, phone call, online chat, text, or video call? If you really need to meet someone, you can prepare all those things that you would like to discuss with them. It will ensure that you can collect all the necessary information in one go without wasting time thinking about things.

Being Choosy While Accepting Invites and Scheduling Appointments

Do you truly need to attend the optional community meeting that will only rehash everything already available on the website? Do you truly need to accept the party invite from a not-so-close friend? It is always a great thing to accept invites when you want to go for it with all your heart. However, when you are not even at it, and it is something that can be canceled without any bad effect, it is better to do so. Before you accept an invite or go for any meeting, try to assess the importance of the same. Also, pay attention to what you want from the core of your heart. Going somewhere where you do not even want to go will not do any good.

Stay Away From Over-Promising or Over-Committing

Do you have the habit of giving away more time than what you can actually afford? Keep in mind that saying "yes" to everything is not cut and dry all the time. For instance, agreeing to arrange a surprise birthday party for a colleague might be a lot more than simply setting up the decorations. It might include inviting people, getting decorations, and so on. Try to be aware of what you are getting into in the true sense. When you feel that you cannot give your time to someone, simply don't.

Preventing the "Should" Syndrome

Do you have the habit of telling yourself, "I should accept the invitation for my friend's birthday/ say yes to their request of helping them out/ complete the new project that the boss asked me to do?" Do you tend to do this on a daily basis without trying to act on your thoughts? All you need to do is either "do" the task or "do not." Or else you will end up wasting your precious time simply by "should"-ing any situation.

14

TIPS FOR SAYING "NO"

Here are some tips that can help you say "no" in situations where you think it is necessary:

Remember Why You Are Saying No

As you are all set to say no, keep in mind why you are even doing it. Try to concentrate on the positive things that it can open up in your life, like more time for your hobbies and family. You will have to say no to things so that you can say yes to all that you want in life. Try to make a list of your priorities and act accordingly.

Disarm and State Your Need

It will get easier for people to accept the "no" from your side when you disarm them first. It can be done by saying that you are flattered and also appreciate their offer, for example. Try to be honest with whatever you say. After this, you can say why you cannot accept their offer this time.

Helping Out a Bit if You Can

In order to leave a conversation where you are trying to say no in a positive way, try to figure out if you can help a bit. You can recommend a person who you think would be a better fit or someone who can help better than you. It will make the other person feel that you are at least trying to help when situations do not permit you.

Adding How You Feel

There are pushy people who might try to overcome all your objections and convince you to do something even when you say no to them. In such instances, you can try to state the way you feel like a reason to say no. For instance, you might say that you do not think the offer is right for you at the moment. Or you can say that your plate is already full, or you feel overwhelmed. So, you cannot accept the offer. The main point of telling a person the way you feel is not to make them understand your issue. It is always hard to argue with the way you feel compared to how you think.

If You Feel Guilty, It Is Okay

Only because you feel guilty for saying no does not indicate that you will need to act on that emotion. Try to be with it instead. As you are with that emotion and let it be, it will start to lose steam after some time. It will keep getting smaller and smaller.

Realize You Cannot Please Some Individuals

It is a fact that you cannot just win over some people. They can never be pleased. It does not matter what you do. It has nothing to do with you but the person himself/herself. Being able to realize this and that you can never make everyone like you even when you say yes can help you stay away from the people-pleasing habit.

Improve Self-Esteem

When you cannot value your own self, you will not be able to value your precious time either. You will need to improve your self-esteem for the betterment of life. When you improve your self-esteem, you can better sense your energy and time. As a result, you would not like to waste it in any way.

CONCLUSION

"I am thankful for all of those who said NO to me. It's because of them I'm doing it myself." – Albert Einstein

Thank you for making it through to the end of *The Art of Saying No;* let's hope it was informative and was able to provide you with all of the tools you need to achieve your goals, whatever they may be.

Saying yes can hurt you in the long run. It can stop you from being productive. Also, building the habit of accepting every offer can impart negative effects on your life. The aim of this guidebook was to make you realize the effects of saying no and how you can do so more often. The tips and tricks that you came across in this guidebook can surely help you change your "yes-man" habit.

When you cannot say no, say that you will try to think about it instead of saying yes or yes with various conditions. You have the right not to have a proper response for anything you are asked for. Provide yourself the time to think when you require too. There is nothing to feel scared about saying no. You will have to learn to do so for your own good. Try it once in the best way possible and see the result. Saying no might feel complex, but it is necessary for a better life ahead.

Finally, if you found this book useful in any way, a review on Amazon is always appreciated, pleasing, and treasured!

CPSIA information can be obtained
at www.ICGtesting.com
Printed in the USA
LVHW022209051222
734629LV00017B/1423

9 781088 071540